TABLE 

QUACKAMOLE ....

GO TO SHELL 2

DOUBLE DOG DARE YA 3

MESS CAR GO 4

THE ROADKILL BLT

      BULLFROGS, LIZZARDS, AND TOADS 5

ROADKILL GOAT, GRITS, GUMBO AND GREENS 6

HOW TO GET CHEAP ROADKILL 8

REDNECK-WHITE TRASH AND BLUE COLLAR BIRDS 9

DON'T DROWND IN YOUR DROOL BROTHER 10

VEGAN STEVEN 12

THE ULTIMATE ROADKILL 14

BIG FOOT BACON 16

MONKEY MAN MEAT LOAF 17

THE CRUNCH'IN LUNCHEON 18

HOOVER HOGS 19

ROADKILL SANDWICH SPREAD 20

THE PRESIDENTIAL ROADKILL PRAYER 21

ROADKILL MONSANTO 23

THROW DOWN WITH BOBBY FLAY 24

"TRIPLE H" HIGHWAYS HOLLERS AND HILLSIDES 25

MAC AND MOUSE 26

KITTY CAT KABOBS 27

FROG WAH 28

OYSTERS THAT ROCKED A FELLER 29

BRAISED & BUTTERED BEEF BRAINS 30

DEER SLIDERS 31

TOM CAT - TOM FLAT 32

POSSUM ON AN OAK PLANK 33

REAL "WILD GAME" RECIPES

POSSUM CASSEROLE 35

HOW TO CATCH A POSSUM 35

WILD POSSUM KABOB 36

POSSUM AND TATERS 37

ARMADILLO IN MUSTARD SAUCE 37

ARMADILLO AND RICE 37

COUNTRY-STYLE GROUNDHOG 38

BAKED GROUND HOG 38

ORIENTAL GROUNDHOG 38

GROUNDHOG AND SWEET POTATOES 39

BAKED SQUIRREL 39

COUNTRY STYLE SQUIRREL 39

OVEN FRIED SQUIRREL 39

BELGIAN SQUIRREL 40

SQUIRREL COUNTRY SAUSAGE 40

GRILLED VENISON BACKSTRAP SUPREME 41

BEST VENISON STIR FRY EVER 41

DEER BURGER KABOB STACKERS 42

COON MEAL IN A BAG (RECIPE 1) 42

COON MEAL IN A BAG (RECIPE 2) 43

BAR-B-Q'D RACCOON 43

MISSISSIPPI COON STEW 43

NEW ORLEANS DOVE RECIPE 44

HOW TO EASILY PLUCK A WILD TURKEY 44

SNAPPING TURTLE IN A POT 44

WILD BOAR BACON 45

WILD BOAR RIBS WITH FIG BBQ SAUCE 45

ABOUT THE FRONT COVER
(BAD EYE)

I BET PEOPLE ARE WONDERING ABOUT THIS FINE MAN

THAT I USED ON THE COVER AS MY ROADKILL MAN

THIS STORY'S TRUE AND YOU REALLY SHOULDN'T DOUBT IT

SO I'LL TAKE JUST A MINUTE AND TELL YOU ABOUT IT

HE'S ONE OF THREE SURVIVORS WHEN THE SILVER BRIDGE FELL

IT'S A STORY THAT MOST OF EM DIDN'T LIVE TO TELL

HE WAS KICKED BY A PONY AND IT TORE UP HIS NOSE

AND NOW IT DON'T WORK RIGHT WHENEVER HE BLOWS

THEN OUT OF THE BLUE AND THIS REALLY SUCKS

HE WAS RUN CLEAN OVER BY A BIG TRASH TRUCK

HE SAID ALL IT REALLY DID WAS SQUASH HIS LEFT KNEE

AND SOME OTHER LITTLE THINGS THAT YOU REALLY CAN'T SEE

HE'S GOT BLACK LUNG FROM MINING AND HAS A LITTLE COUGH

THEN WAS HIT ON HIS HARLEY AND CUT HIS GOOD LEG OFF

HE WENT TO JUMP A BATTERY AND IT BLEW SKY HIGH

IT BURNED UP HIS FACE AND PUT OUT HIS EYE

MOST FOLK WOULD GIVE UP AND JUST SIT THERE AND SOB

HE'S GOT ONE BAD EYE BUT HE CAN STILL FIND A JOB

SO IF YOU'VE GOT A PROBLEM WITH THIS FINE MAN

REPRESENTING MT BOOK AS THE ROADKILL MAN

JUST REMEMBER HALF THE COUNTRY IS RECEIVING A CHECK

BUT BAD EYE WORKS EVEN THOUGH HE'S A WRECK

QUACKAMOLE

ONE DAY I WAS DRIVIN' DOWN THE ROAD IN MY TRUCK

AND RIGHT OUT OF NOWHERE HERE FLEW A DUCK

THE DUCK LOST CONTROL AND FLEW INTO MY FENDER

I PLUCKED ALL HIS FEATHERS AND PUT HIM IN THE BLENDER

I LEFT ALL THE GUTS IN AND DON'T THINK THAT I'M MEAN

BUT WHEN I TURNED ON THE BLENDER THE MIXTURE
    TURNED GREEN

I LEFT HIS FEET INTACT AND I LEFT ON HIS QUACKER

SO THIS RECIPE WOULD RHYME WHEN I DIPPED IN MY
    CRACKER

THIS STUFF IS SO GOOD YOU'LL DO A BACK FLIP

YOU CAN DIP IT WITH CRACKERS OR TORTILLA CHIPS

YOU CAN MAKE QUACKAMOLE IN JUST A VERY SHORT TIME

AND I'M SO PROUD TO SAY THAT THIS RECIPES MINE

GO TO SHELL

IF YA DON'T LIKE THE NORMAL ROADKILL MEAT

LIKE POSSUMS AND COONS AND SKUNKS OF THE STREET

WELL I'M SORRY TO HEAR THAT ALRIGHT-OH WELL

AS FAR AS I'M CONCERNED YOU CAN GO STRAIGHT TO SHELL

ALL THIS I SAY IN A VERY POSITIVE WAY

CAUSE TURTLES COME OUT AROUND HERE ABOUT MAY

SEE TURTLES HAVE THE VERY BEST OF ANY KIND OF MEAT

THEY'RE THE VERY BEST CRITTER YOU CAN FIND ON THE STREET

THERE'S SOFT SHELL AND SNAPPER AND BOX TURTLE STEW

I'M GONNA TELL YA HOW TO FIX'EM – HERE'S WHAT YA DO

THEY'RE KIND OF LIKE A LOBSTER YA COOK THE THINGS LIVE

AND YOU CAN ADD A LITTLE HONEY FROM YOUR HONEY BEE HIVE

JUST LAY'EM UPSIDE DOWN IN YOUR PRESSURE COOKER DUDE

IF THEY'RE LITTLE BITTY TURTLES YOU SHOULD COOK QUITE A FEW

EVEN GRANDMA CAN CATCH'EM WHEN THEY'RE OUT ON THE

    ROAD

AND THEY'RE EASY TO CATCH IN YOUR YARD WHEN YOU'VE

    MOWED

ME AND MY YOUNG'INS HAVE CAUGHT QUITE A FEW

AND IF THEY BITE OFF THEIR FINGER I COOK IT UP TOO

I JUST ADD A LITTLE STOCK FROM CHICKEN OR A COW

ADD SOME CELERY AND GARLIC AND THERE IT IS-WOW!

DOUBLE DOG DARE YA

TWO DOGS GOT KILLED EATIN A ROADKILL COON

THAT GOT SQUASHED ON THE ROAD BY THE LIGHT OF THE MOON

IT WAS A LITTLE LATE WHEN I KICKED ON MY BRIGHTS

I HIT BOTH OF THOSE DOGS AND I CRIED THAT NIGHT

BUT RATHER THAN LET THOSE DOGS GO TO WASTE

I GATHERED THEM UP TO SEE HOW THEY WOULD TASTE

TEARS FLOWED DOWN AS I SKINNED THE DOGS OUT

CAUSE I'M A DOG LOVIN' MAN THERE AIN'T NO DOUBT

SO I STARTED THIS RECIPE THAT DAY AROUND NOON

AND I DID GATHER UP WHAT WAS LEFT OF THAT COON

I WENT TO THE CABINET AND GOT A NUMBER 8 SKILLET

AND CUT THE DOG MEAT UP AND BEGAN TO FILL IT

I PUT IN SOME FLOUR AND A WHOLE STICK OF BUTTER

THAT'S HOW TO COOK A DOG ACCORDING TO MY MOTHER

TURN THE HEAT UP HIGH AND STIR IN SOME MILK

STIR OUT THE LUMPS UNTILL IT TURNS SMOOTH AS SILK

THEN YA TAKE IT OFF THE STOVE AND PUT IT IN THE OVEN

AND GO PET YOUR DOG AND GIVE HIM SOME LOVIN'

JUST LEAVE IT IN THE OVEN ABOUT AN HOUR AND A HALF

AND IT'LL TURN REAL TENDER LIKE MEAT FROM A CALF

THIS IS REAL GOOD EATIN' NO MATTER HOW YA FEEL

AND I DOUBLE DOG DARE YA TO TRY THIS MEAL

MESS CAR GO

ES CAR GO IS JUST A FANCY NAME FOR SNAIL

AND THEY GO REAL GOOD WITH SOME COLLARD GREENS OR KALE

YOU'LL KNOW WHEN YA HIT ONE CAUSE THEY MAKE A POPPIN'
    SOUND

AND THEN YA STOP YUR CAR AND GO LOOKIN' AROUND

JUST SCRAPE'EM OFF THE ROAD-A LITTLE PUDDY KNIFE WILL DO

TO GET YOURSELF A MESS OF'EM IT TAKES QUITE A FEW

I USE A BUTTER SAUCE WITH WINE AND SOME GARLIC WITH HERBS

I CAN'T EXPLAIN HOW GOOD IT IS WITH PLAIN 'OLE WORDS

THE PRESENTATIONS' PRETTY UGLY AND IT LOOKS LIKE A MESS

BUT THE RECIPE IS TASTY IT'S ONE OF MY BEST

JUST MELT A POUND OF BUTTER OVER MEDIUM HEAT

AND ADD A CUP OF WINE AND ALL YUR SNAIL MEAT

ADD SOME HERBS AND SALT AND PEPPER AND SERVE IT IN A BOWL

AND THERE YA GO YA GOT IT MAN "A MESS CAR GO"

THE ROADKILL BLT
BULLFROGS, LIZZARDS, AND TOADS

WITH ALL THE GOOD CRITTERS YOU CAN FIND ON THE ROAD

DON'T FORGET THE BULLFROGS, LIZZARDS, AND TOADS

THERE'S NOT MUCH TO'EM- NOT MORE THAN A BITE

BUT I GUARANTEE YA ONE THING THEY SURE TASTE RIGHT

YA TAKE TWO OR THREE LIZZARDS SOME TOADS AND A FROG

AND PUT'EM ON A BISCUIT AND GIVE ONE TO YOUR DOG

YA DON'T SKIN'EM OR GUT'EM CAUSE THEY GOT NO HAIR

OR YA CAN IF YA WANT TO I DON'T CARE

SOME PEOPLE FRY'EM IN SOME REALLY HOT GREASE

JUST TEST IT ON A LIZZARD AND TRY A LITTLE PIECE

BUT I JUST LIKE TO EAT THE DANG THINGS RAW

ON A BIG BUTTERED BISCUIT OH YEAH-YEE HAW

THE BEST THING ABOUT IT IS THERE OFF THE ROAD AND
     THEY'RE FREE

AND I KNOW YOU'LL NEVER HAVE A BETTER BLT

ROADKILL GOAT, GRITS, GUMBO AND GREENS

GOOD GOLLY MOLLY OH MAN WHAT A MEAL

THIS STUFF WILL MAKE YA BETTER NO MATTER HOW BAD YA FEEL

THE FIRST GOAT I EVER ATE WE WERE BOTH JUST KIDS

NO PUN INTENDED BUT HERE'S WHAT I DID

I WAS RIDIN' DOWN THE ROAD REAL FAST ON MY BIKE

I COULDN'T SEE REAL GOOD CAUSE IT WAS REAL LATE AT NIGHT

I HIT SOMETHING REAL HARD-IT MADE ME WRECK AND I FELL

I HIT A LITTLE GOAT AND KILLED IT DEADER THAN HELL

I WAS ALL SKINNED UP ON MY ELBOWS AND KNEES

MY BIKE WAS TORE UP AND IT WAS TOO DARK TO SEE

SO THERE I STOOD BLEEDIN' IN THE ROAD ALL ALONE

I GRABBED THE GOAT BY THE EAR AND DRUG THE THING HOME

WHEN I GOT THERE I SKINNED IT AND HUNG IT IN THE SHED

I TOLD MOMMA I WAS HOME AND WENT STRAIGHT TO BED

YOU CAN WORK UP A GOAT LOTS OF DIFFERENT WAYS

BUT I LET MINE HANG 'BOUT THREE OR FOUR DAYS

I CUT SOME LITTLE STEAKS FROM THE LOINS AND THE HINDS

I CAN CUT IT LIKE I WANT TO-THE DANG GOATS MINE

BUT THE REAL PRIZE MEAT IS RIGHT AROUND THE THROAT

CAUSE THAT'S WHAT I USE TO MAKE MY GUMBO GOAT

I'M SORRY TO TELL YOU AFTER ALL THIS GAB

THAT I LOST THE ORIGINAL RECIPE I HAD

BUT MOMMA SAID HEY- IT'S STILL A GOOD POEM

IF THEY WANTA KNOW HOW TO MAKE IT YOU'LL JUST HAVE TO

    SHOW'EM

ALL MY FRIENDS UP THE HOLLER-THEY'RE ALL A BUNCH OF

    GRITS

AND I INVITED'EM DOWN AND LET'EM EAT A LITTLE BIT

BUT I WILL TELL YA THIS-IT GOES REALLY GOOD WITH GREENS

FRIED PEPPERS AND CORN AND HALF RUNNER BEANS

HOW TO GET CHEAP ROADKILL

IF YA WANNA SAVE MONEY CAUSE THE PRICE OF GAS IS HIGH

I'VE GOTA GOOD IDEA A LITTLE SOMETHING YOU CAN TRY

YOU SHOULD'T HAVE TO TRAVEL VERY FAR DOWN THE ROAD

TO FIND A DEER OR A POSSUM OR A LITTLE BITTY TOAD

SO GO OUT ON THE HIGHWAY AND STEAL YOURSELF SOME SIGNS

NOT THE ONES THAT SAY STOP I MEAN THE DEER CROSSING KIND

PUT IT UP IN YOUR DRIVEWAY THAT LEADS UP TO YOUR TRAILER

AND WHEN A DEER COMES OUT WELL THAT'S WHEN YA NAIL'ER

YOU GET YOUR ROADKILL THIS A WAY AND NEVER LEAVE THE

HOLLER AND YOUR TOTAL COST FOR YOUR GASOLINE WILL

BE ABOUT A DOLLAR

THEN YA FRY A HUNK OF MEAT AND

THROW IT ON SOME BREAD

IT'S THE CHEAPEST WAY I

KNOW TO KEEP YOUR KIDS

AND FAMILY FED

REDNECK-WHITE TRASH AND BLUE COLLAR BIRDS

REDNECK, WHITE TRASH AND BLUE COLLAR BIRDS

HERE'S HOW YA MAKE IT IN SO MANY WORDS

TAKE SOME RED BIRDS AND PIGEONS AND AN OLD MALLARD
DUCK

THAT YA PULL OUT FROM UNDERNEATH YOUR JACKED UP
TRUCK

YA CUT ALL THE FEET OFF AND PUT EM IN A PAN

LET EM SIMMER WITH THE LID ON AND THEN LET EM STAND

THIS WILL MAKE A THICK AND TASTY BIRD FOOT BROTH

YOU CAN SEASON WITH SOME BUTTERFLIES SOME GARLIC AND
A MOTH

IF YA THROW IN THE TONGUES THE BIRDS WILL SURELY TASTE
BETTER

BE SURE TO FOLLOW THIS RECIPE EXACTLY TO THE LETTER

YOU CAN SKIN EM OUT OR PLUCK EM IT DON'T MATTER WHAT
YA DO

JUST DON'T PEAK AT THEIR BREAST BOY- SHAME ON YOU

THEN MARINADE THE BIRDIE MEAT IN SOME FINE RED WINE

YOU CAN DRINK ALL THAT'S LEFT I DO IT ALL THE TIME

BROWN THE MEAT IN A SKILLET WITH SOME E.V.O.O.

ADD THE BROTH AND SOME CARROTS STICKS AND COOK IT
REAL SLOW

THIS RECIPE IS REALLY GOOD AND ALSO TELLS THE STORY

OF THE BIRDIE RECIPE NAMED AFTER OLE GLORY

DON'T DROWND IN YOUR DROOL BROTHER

THERE'S NEVER BEEN A BETTER COOK THAN MY DEAR SWEET

    LOVING MOTHER

AND AT TIMES IT CAUSES FIST FIGHTS AT THE TABLE WITH MY

    BROTHER

THE LAST TIME MAMA COOKED A MEAL WE FOUGHT LIKE

    DRUNK'IN SAILORS

AND I THREW MY BROTHER THROUGH THE WALL OF MY LOVING

    MOTHERS TRAILER

SO NOW WHEN MAMA COOKS A MEAL WE HAVE TO WAIT OUTSIDE

AND SHE CALLS US ONE BY ONE TO EAT THE ROADKILL THAT SHE

    FRIED

SHE BASES IT ON BEHAVIOR AS TO WHO SHE WOULD CALL FIRST

AND SINCE I'M MY MOMMIES SWEETY PIE I WAS ALWAYS CHOSEN

    FIRST

ONE DAY SHE COOKED SOME COLLARD GREENS WITH SOME

GROUND HOG THAT SHE FRIED

AS I ATE I WATCHED MY BROTHER DROOL STANDING THERE

    OUTSIDE

HE COULD'NT HARDLY STAND IT AS HE STOOD AND WATCHED ME

    SAVOR IT

I KNEW COLLARD GREENS AND GROUND HOG MEAT WERE MY

    BROTHERS FAVORITE

HE WEEPED AND WHALED AND NASH'ED HIS TEETH AND AT HIS

    FEET WAS A POOL

THE PRESSURE WAS MORE THAN HE COULD BARE AND HE

    DROWNDED IN HIS DROOL

WHEN I FINISHED UP MY SUPPER I LAYED THE BOY TO REST

I SAVED A PIECE OF GROUND HOG MEAT TO LAY UPON HIS CHEST

BECAUSE I'M MOMMIES SWEETIE PIE - THAT'S THE REASON THAT

    HE'S DEAD

SO MAMA CARVED THE BOY A STONE AND THIS IS WHAT IT SAID

"HERE LIES MY TEENAGE SON

HE WAS ALWAYS NUMBER TWO

HE GRADUATED SECOND GRADE IN ELEMENTRY SCHOOL

ALL HE EVER ASKED OF ME WAS LOVE AND TO BE FED

BUT BECAUSE OF POOR BEHAVIOR

HE DROWN IN DROOL INSTEAD"

VEGAN STEVEN

ONCE UPON A TIME THERE WAS A MAN NAMED VEGAN STEVEN

AND EVERYBODY LIKED HIM MOST WHEN STEVEN WAS A LEAV'IN

STEVE DRANK LOTS OF WHISKEY AND THEN WOULD DRIVE HIS CAR

AND STEVEN SPENT A LOT OF TIME DOWN AT THE LOCAL BAR

VEGAN STEVEN WOULD'NT LEAVE TILL HE'D SPENT ALL OF HIS

   DOLLARS

THEN HE'D JUMP BACK IN HIS CAR AND DRIVE IT UP THE HOLLER

AND THE REASON VEGAN STEVEN'S VEGAN IS CAUSE HE'S

   LEAV'IN HEAV'IN AND WEAV'IN

NOW VEGAN STEVEN'S WIFE IS GRIEV'IN AND THE ROADS

   WERE'NT EVEN AT LEAST TO STEVEN

SO VEGAN STEVEN'S SEE'IN DOUBLE AND GOT IN TROUBLE CAUSE

   HE HIT A BIG BUCK DEER

IT CAME THROUGH THE GLASS REALLY FAST AND SPILLED ALL

   STEVEN'S BEER

THERE WAS NO PLEAS'IN VEGAN STEVEN TILL HE WAS LEAV'IN

   HEAV'IN AND WEAV'IN AND THE ROADS WERE'NT EVEN AT

   LEAST TO STEVEN WITH ANTLERS THROUGH HIS HEAD

AND THE ONLY REASON VEGAN STEVEN'S VEGAN IS CAUSE HE

   WAS LEAV'IN DRUNK AND WEAV'IN AND HEAV'IN AND NOW

   HIS WIFE IS REALLY GRIEV'IN BECAUSE VEGAN STEVEN'S DEAD

AND IF YOU DRINK LIKE VEGAN STEVEN AND PLAN ON LEAV'IN

HEAV'N AND WEAV'IN AND THINK IT'S PLEAS'IN TO HAVE

YOUR WIFE A GRIEV'IN IT'S MORE THAN I'M CONCEIV'N

BUT I'M NOT BELIEV'IN THAT YOUR CONCIEV'IN THAT YOU'D

WANT TO BE LIKE VEGAN STEVEN LEAV'IN THE BAR A

WEAV'IN AND HEAV'IN AND SEND YOUR WIFE A GRIEV'IN

AND THINK IT'S PLEAS'IN LIKE VEGAN STEVEN

THE ULTIMATE ROADKILL

I WAS DRIV'IN HOME REAL LATE ONE NIGHT AS I USUALLY
    ALWAYS WOULD

WHEN I MADE THE TURN OFF GARFIELD ROAD I LOOKED AND
    THERE IT STOOD

AT FIRST I THOUGHT IT WAS BRIAN SIMS BUT THIS APE WAS THREE
    FOOT TALLER

AND I COULD SEE IT TORE UP QUITE A PATCH WHERE IT RAMBLED
    OUT THE HOLLER

COULD THIS BE A GREAT BIG MONKEY THAT CLIMBED OFF OF
    SOMEONES BACK

WHEN IT SCREAMED THE CHILLS WENT UP MY SPINE & BOUT
    CAUSED A HEART ATTACK

WHEN I HIT MY BRAKES TO MISS THE THING I WENT INTO A SPIN

BUT IT CAUGHT THE BUMPER OF MY TRUCK AND TORE IT OFF
    AGAIN

I NEVER THOUGHT I'D SEE THIS THING ON THESE ROADS A LURK'IN

IT LAYED THERE DY'IN IN THE ROAD A TWITCH'IN AND A JERK'IN

WHEN I GOT OUT I SMELLED THE THING - WHAT AN AWFUL STINCH

IT WAS WAY TO BIG TO CARRY HOME SO I DRUG IT WITH MY
    WINCH

I COULD'NT HELP BUT NOTICE THE MASSIVE SIZE OF THIS THINGS
    FEET

AND MY ESTIMATED HANG'IN WEIGHT WAS A THOUSAND POUNDS
    OF MEAT

I TOOK THE HIDE AND SALTED IT AND SPREAD IT OUT TO DRY

AND I CUT A HUNK OF TENDERLOIN FOR MAW TO COOK AND TRY

I CALLED A BUNCH OF FRIENDS OF MINE FOR THEM TO TAKE A PEEK

I SAID I'D KILLED A MONKEY MAN WITH TWO GREAT BIG HUGE FEET

THEN A BUNCH OF PRESS CAME OUT AND SOME DUDES FROM A
    MUSEUM

AND PEOPLE CAME FROM EVERYWHERE JUST TO COME AND SEE HIM

THEY ALL TOOK SOME PHOTOS OF IT - A HANG'IN THERE A CHILL'N

AS I PATTIED OUT SOME BURGERS AND WAS DRINK'IN BEER AND
    GRILL'IN

ONE GUY OFFERED FIFTY GRAND FOR MY NINE FOOT MONKEY MAN

I TOOK THE CASH BUT KEPT ALL OF THE BACONS AND THE HAMS

SO IF YOUR OUT AND DRIV'IN DOWN THE ROAD AND HIT AN APE

IT'S WORTH YOUR WHILE TO WORK IT UP EVEN IF IT'S LATE

IF YOU WANT TO TRY SOME BIG FOOT MEAT AND HAVE NO RECIPE

DON'T FORGET WHO'S WRIT'IN THIS JUST TURN THE PAGE AND SEE

BIG FOOT BACON

YOU'LL NEED A FEW INGREDIANTS TO MAKE A BIG FOOT BACON

DEPEND'IN ON THE SIZE OF HIM AND HOW MUCH YOU'LL BE

    MAK'IN

IF YOUR BIG FOOT'S NINE FOOT TALL LIKE THE ONE I KILLED THAT

    NIGHT

JUST DOUBLE UP THIS RECIPE IF YA WANNA MAKE IT RIGHT

GET SOME SALT AND SUGAR AND JUST ADD A PINCH OF CURE

AND GET SOME GREAT BIG VATS TO SOAK IT IN FOR SURE

THEN MIX ALL YOUR INGREDIANTS THAT I MENTIONED UP ABOVE

THEN STIR IT IN WITH WATER FOR YOUR BRINE AND ADD SOME

    LOVE

LET IT SIT FOR SEVERAL DAYS AND STIR FROM TIME TO TIME

JUST SLICE IT UP AND FRY IT MAN - WOW THIS BACONS FINE

MONKEY MAN MEAT LOAF

TO MAKE A BIG FOOT MEATLOAF IS SO EASY AND IT'S FUN

AND YOU'LL BE SO GLAD YOU COOKED IT, WHEN YOUR MONKEY

    MEATLOAF'S DONE

GRIND A LITTLE BIG FOOT MEAT, YOU'LL NEED THREE POUNDS OF

    GROUND

CHOP SOME ONIONS AND SOME PEPPERS AND IN A SKILLET

    SWEAT'EM DOWN

I LIKE TO USE THE EXCESS MEAT I TRIMMED OFF BIG FOOTS KNEES

ADD A COUPLE GARLIC CLOVES AND GRATED COLBY CHEESE

THEN ADD A LITTLE BREAD CRUMBS - SMELLS GREAT TO SAY THE

    LEAST

IT'S AMAZING WHAT A MEATLOAF YOU CAN MAKE FROM SUCH A

    BEAST

THEN JUST STICK IT IN THE OVEN AND YA COOK IT FOR AN HOUR

YOU CAN RUB IT WITH SOME SUGAR IF YA THINK YOUR

    MEATLOAFS SOUR

THEN TAKE IT OUT AND LET IT REST WHEN YOU THINK YOUR

    MEATLOAF'S DONE

YOU CAN SLICE IT UP AND SERVE IT ON A TOASTED HOAGIE BUN

THE CRUNCH'IN LUNCHEON

HERE'S A WAY TO GET A DEER I BET YOU AIN'T THOUGHT OF

JUST GO DOWN TO THE HARDWARE STORE AND BUY A RUBBER

    GLOVE

THEN PICK YA UP A JUG OR TWO OF GOOD OLE DOE IN HEAT

THEN DRIVE OUT ON A COUNTRY ROAD DON'T USE A CITY STREET

THEN SOAK YOUR BUMPER LIBERALLY USING DOE PEE WITH YOUR

    GLOVE

THEN LET YOUR MOTOR RADIATE THAT SCENT OF BOTTLED LOVE

THEN JUST SIT THERE IDLING NO NEED TO REV YOUR MOTOR

CAUSE BUCKS FROM SEVERAL MILES AWAY WILL RECOGNIZE

    THAT ODER

THEN JUST SIT THERE PATIENTLY WITH YOUR RIGHT FOOT ON THE

    GAS

CAUSE WHEN THEY COME A HUNCH'IN MAN YOU'LL WANNA

    FLOOR IT FAST

THIS SAVES YOU MONEY AND YOUR TIME JUST SIT THERE IN THE

    ROAD

IT'S THE FASTEST WAY TO GET A DEER I THINK I'VE EVER KNOWED

HOOVER HOGS

I MET A MAN FROM ALABAM IN A BEER JOINT IN THE SOUTH

HE WAS DRINK'IN BEER AND TELL'IN JOKES WITH OYSTERS IN HIS
    MOUTH

HE HAD A BIG TALL 4 WHEEL DRIVE AND THE BACK WAS FULL OF
    DOGS

AND HE SAID HE HUNTED HALF THE NIGHT AND CAUGHT SOME
    HOOVER HOGS

WHAT THE HECK'S A HOOVER HOG? I SAT THERE AND I THOUGHT

WHAT KIND OF CREATURE WAS IT THAT HIS HOOVER HOG DOGS
    HAD CAUGHT

HE SAID BACK IN THE THIRTIES, WHEN HOOVER WAS OUR CHIEF

WE STARTED CATCH'IN HOOVER HOGS - THAT'S ALL THERE WAS
    TO EAT

WALK OUTSIDE AND TAKE A LOOK BUT WATCH
    OUT FOR MY DOGS

AND IN A BAG WERE
    SEVERAL OF WHAT HE
    CALLED HOOVER HOGS

SOMETIMES IT'S HARD TO
    GET THESE CRAZY
    RECIPES TO RHYME

BUT ALL HE HAD WAS
    POSSUMS, HECK I
    CATCH'EM ALL THE TIME

ROADKILL SANDWICH SPREAD

EVERYONE HAS SEEN THE DEER OUT ON OUT ON THE INTERSTATE

WHERE A TRACTOR TRAILER WAS THE WAY IT MET IT'S UGLY

    FATE

THERE'S A REALLY BIG RED UGLY SMEAR SPREAD UP AND DOWN

    THE ROAD

YA HATE TO SEE IT HAPPEN BUT THAT'S THE WAY IT GOES

YA USE DEER LIKE THIS THAT ARE REALLY REALLY DEAD

TO MAKE THIS FANCY RECIPE CALLED ROADKILL SANDWICH

    SPREAD

AT THE END OF THE SMEAR YOU'LL FIND A LITTLE PILE OF MEAT

AND IT'S ALREADY BLENDED IN WITH HEAD HIDE AND FEET

IF IT'S LAYED A GOOD WHILE IN THE REAL HOT AUGUST SUN

IT MIGHT BE COOKED ENOUGH AND BE ALREADY DONE

IF IT'S NOT DONE ON THE ROAD WELL DON'T SWEAT IT MAN

JUST TAKE IT HOME AND THROW IT IN A SKILLET OR A PAN

THEN YA SEASON THE SPREAD WITH SOME ANCHOVIE PASTE

ADD YOUR FAVORITE SPICES AND SOME GARLIC SALT FOR TASTE

I LIKE TO SERVE IT OPEN FACED ON SOME TOASTED WHITE BREAD

IT MAKES A FANTASTIC SNACK RIGHT BEFORE YA GO TO BED

THE PRESIDENTIAL ROADKILL PRAYER

BEFORE YOU EAT ANY MEAL THERE'S SOMETHING YOU SHOULD DO

AND THAT'S ASK YOUR GOD IN HEAVEN TO BLESS ALL OF YOUR

     FOOD

BUT WHEN I WENT TO THE WHITE HOUSE FOR THE YEARLY

     ROADKILL FEAST

I SAT BESIDE THREE JEWISH MEN EIGHT MUSLIMS AND A PRIEST

JUST A COUPLE OF TABLES OVER THERE WAS AN ATHEISTIC MAN

A GROUP OF NEW AGE PEOPLE AND A MAN FROM PAKISTAN

AND WHEN THEY BROUGHT THE POSSUM AND THE ARMADILLO

     STEW

SOMEONE STARTED AN ARGUMENT AS TO WHO WOULD BLESS THE

     FOOD

ONE MAN STOOD UP AND SCREAMED-I'LL KILL ALL YOU INFADELS

WHILE ANOTHER PULLED A PISTOL AND SAID I'LL SEND YOU ALL

     TO HELL

YET ANOTHER DROPPED HIS PANTS AND YELLED HE WAS GONNA

     KILL THE JEWS

WHEN HE PULLED A CORD HIS BUTT BLEW OFF AND IT LANDED IN

     THE STEW

ONE MAN STOOD COMPLAINING THAT HE HATED POSSUM FRIED

AND THE PRESIDENT GRABBED A POSSUM BONE AND STUCK IT IN

     HIS EYE

THEN SOMEONE IN THE BACK YELLED OUT- I'LL PRAY ABOUT THE
    FOOD

CAUSE I'M A NEW AGE BABTASTOLIC METHAPALIAN JEW

THEN THE ATHEISTIC MAN YELLED OUT - I CAN'T BELIEVE YOU
    GUYS

WITH ALL YOUR BOMBS AND GUNS AND THINGS AND POSSUM
    BONES IN EYES

SO THIS IS WHAT WERE GONNA DO- JUST FORGET ABOUT THE
    PRAYER

IT'S THE ONLY WAY TO DO THIS THING AND BE COMPLETELY FAIR

SO WITH THAT SAID THEY ALL WERE FED & WERE FEELING
    REALLY MEEK

AND THE CHRISTIAN GRABBED THE BLOWN OFF BUTT AND
    TURNED THE OTHER CHEEK

THREE MUSLIMS GAVE COMMUNION TO THE HINDU BUDIST JEW

AND TOGETHER THEY HAD PICTURES MADE ALL SITTING ON A PEW

SO THEY ATE THE ARMADILLO STEW AND ATE THE POSSUM FRIED

BUT SINCE NO ONE REALLY BLESSED THE FOOD THEY ALL GOT
    SICK AND DIED

ROADKILL MONSANTO

HAVE YOU TRIED ROADKILL MONSANTO - HEY WHAT A TASTEY
    TREAT

THEY SAY ITS STILL REALLY SAFE EVEN THOUGH IT HAS SIX FEET

GENETIC MODIFICATION MAKES IT BETTER ANYWAY

YOUR MEAT STAYS FRESH OUT ON THE ROAD FOR 6 OR 7 DAYS

IT MAKES ROADKILL MORE NUTRITIOUS AT LEAST THAT'S WHAT
    THEY SAID

BUT IT MAKES ME KINDA WONDER WHY MY KIDS HAVE WEIRD
    SHAPED HEADS

THE TASTE IS SO MUCH BETTER NOW, ALL ROADKILLS' FINGER
    LICKIN'

CAUSE SINCE THEIR SUPER HYBRIDYZED THEY ALL TASTE JUST
    LIKE CHICKEN

THE BEST WAY YOU CAN COOK IT IS TO COOK IT LOW AND SLOW

AND IF YOU ADD SOME BUTTERMILK IT HELPS TONE DOWN THE
    GLOW

YOU CAN SPREAD IT ON A PIZZA OR PUT IT ON A BUN

JUST SERVE IT WITH SOME SOY BEANS AND HAVE A LOT OF FUN

THROW DOWN WITH BOBBY FLAY

HAVE YOU EVER SEEN THE THROW DOWN SHOW STARRING
    BOBBY FLAY

WELL HE SHOWED UP IN MY KITCHEN WITH SOME ROADKILL
    YESTERDAY

TH E THROW DOWN WAS WITH RACOON MEAT, THAT'S WHAT WE
    WERE TO COOK

I TOOK HIS CHALLENGE RIGHT AWAY CAUSE HEY I WROTE THE
    BOOK

I HAD TO HELP OUT BOBBY FLAY CAUSE HE COULD'NT SKIN HIS
    COON

AND WE STOOD COOKING IN MY KITCHEN UNTIL LATE THAT
    AFTERNOON

HE MADE A CALIFORNIA COMPOTE SERVED WITH COLETTES OF
    THE MEAT

BUT I MADE RACOON CROQUETTE SERVED WITH CREVETTES
    FROM THE CREEK

WHEN THE JUDGES ATE MY
    RACOON DISH THEY WERE
    DANC'IN ALL AROUND

BUT WHEN THE JUDGES ATE
    BOBBY'S COON THEY THREW
    IT ON THE GROUND

"TRIPLE H"
HIGHWAYS HOLLERS
AND HILLSIDES

EVERYONE'S HEARD OF TRIPLE D, THAT SHOW WITH GUY FIETTI

HE WATCHES PEOPLE COOK THEIR MEALS LIKE BURGERS AND

    SPAGHETTI

GUY WILL TRAVEL EVERYWHERE ACROSS OUR FIFTY STATES

BUT NOW I HAVE A BRAND NEW SHOW AND I CALL IT TRIPLE H

I GO AROUND THE COUNTRY ON THE HIGHWAYS AND THE ROADS

AND I GATHER UP ALL THE ROADKILL - FROM A MOOSE DOWN TO

    A TOAD

I GO UP ALL THE HOLLERS AND ALL THE HILLS THERE IN BETWEEN

AND DID I MENTION IT'S ORGANIC, AND REALLY REALLY LEAN

THEN I TAKE IT HOME AND COOK SOME TASTEY RECIPES

AND IT'S TELEVISED THROUGH SATALITE FOR ALL THE WORLD TO

    SEE

MAC AND MOUSE

I DON'T REALLY KNOW WHERE I'M GOING WITH THIS YET

BUT IF YA GIVE ME TEN MINUTES I'D BE WILLING TO BET

THAT I CAN QUIT SITTIN' HERE THINKING OUT LOUD

AND MAKE UP A RECIPE TO PLEASE THE WHOLE CROWD

YA JUST COOK YOUR MACARONI LIKE YA ALWAYS DO

AFTER YOU'VE SAVED UP YOUR MICE FOR A MONTH OR TWO

YA JUST STIR FRY THE MICE ON THE STOVE IN A WOK

I COULD SURE THINK BETTER IF THE KIDS DIDN'T TALK

STIR FRY IT HARD OVER REAL HIGH HEAT

THROW SOME GARLIC AND SALT IN TO FLAVOR THE MEAT

THEN THROW A LITTLE LIQUOR IN I USE ABOUT A CUP

AND STRIKE A MATCH REAL QUICK AND LIGHT THE MICE UP

THEN THROW A LITTLE BUTTER IN AND STIR IN SOME FLOUR

AND LET IT SIMMER AND THICKEN FOR ALOMOST AN HOUR

BY NOW YOU CAN SMELL IT ALL OVER THE HOUSE

MIX IT ALL TOGETHER AND THERE'S YOUR MAC AND MOUSE

KITTY CAT KABOBS

FIND YOURSELF A KITTY DEAD ON THE STREET

I KNOW WHAT YOUR THINK'IN BUT IT'S REALLY GOOD MEAT

THEY SAY THERE'S MORE THAN ONE WAY TO SKIN OUT A CAT

BUT I SKIN'EM LIKE A POSSUM OR SOMETHING LIKE THAT

BUY A PAK OF SKEWER STICKS FROM DOWN AT THE STORE

IF YA FIND TWO OR THREE CATS YOU'LL HAVE TO BUY MORE

ONCE YA CHOP UP YOUR KITTY CAT YOUR JUST ABOUT READY

YA PUT'EM ON THE SKEWER STICKS AND ALTERATE WITH VEGGIES

YOU CAN SOAK'EM IN A MARINADE FOR JUST ABOUT A DAY

OR PUT EM ON YOUR BBQ AND COOK'EM THAT A WAY

I KNOW IT'S A SHAME THAT THE KITTY CAT WAS KILLED

BUT LOOK AT IT ON THE BRIGHT SIDE-YOUR BELLY GOT FILLED

FROG WAH

WHAT A BIG FANCY FRENCH WORD WELL LA-TI-DA

THEY COOK THE LIVER FROM A GOOSE AND THEY CALL IT FRAGUA

THEY CHARGE BIG MONEY FOR AN OLE GOOSES GUTS

BUT I ALWAYS FED IT TO MY COON DOG PUPS

SO I DECIDED ONE DAY THAT I WOULD PROVE A POINT

THAT YA DON'T NEED TO GO TO A FANCY FRENCH JOINT

JUST STOP AND GET SOME ROADKILL JUST ANY KIND OF CRITTER

AND STICK YOUR HAND RIGHT IN HIS GUTS AND FIND THE

      CRITTERS LIVER

YOU CAN USE THE LIVER FROM A COON OR A POSSUM OR DOG

BUT I JUST DECIDED THAT I WOULD TRY FROGS

SO I GOT ME SOME FROGS AND I MEAN A WHOLE BUNCH

I ATE THE BODYS FOR MY BREAKFAST AND SAVED THE LIVERS FOR

      MY LUNCH

YA JUST FILL A SKILLET WITH LIVERS AND TURN IT ON LOW

AND LET THE FAT SEEP OUT OF THE LIVERS REAL SLOW

SO LISTEN UP CLOSELY CAUSE HERES WHAT I DID

I TOOK THE SKILLET OFF THE STOVE AND SET IT IN THE FRIG

AND IN JUST A LITTLE BIT IT TURNED INTO A JELLY

IT DON'T COST A DANG THING AND TASTES GOOD IN YOUR BELLY

OYSTERS THAT ROCKED A FELLER

ARE THEY OYSTERS OR CLAMS I'M NOT SURE WHAT THEY ARE

BUT AT LEAST I DIDN'T HAVE TO HIT'EM WITH MY CAR

I WAS STANDIN' THERE FISHIN' AND I HAD TO TAKE A LEAK

AND I SPOTTED A BUNCH OF'EM LAY'IN IN THE CREEK

THEY WERE ALL JUST LAYING THERE RIGHT ON THE BOTTOM

SO I WADED IN THE WATER AND WRETCHED DOWN AND GOT'EM

I DIDN'T KNOW WHETHER TO COOK'EM OR EAT THE THINGS RAW

SO I PRYED A COUPLE OPEN AND HERE'S WHAT I SAW

THE DANG THANGS STUNK LIKE OLD DIRTY SOCKS

AND THE FIRST ONE I OPENED I SLUNK IT ON A ROCK

BUT SOME LITTLE CRITTERS ARE AN ACQUIRED TASTE

SO I ATE A DOZEN OF'EM CAUSE I DON'T LIKE TO WASTE

I HAVE OFTEN HEARD IT SAID THAT THEY ARE AN APHRODESIAC

SO I TOOK A DOZEN FOR MY WIFE TO EAT BACK AT THE SHACK

THAT NIGHT WE HAD FUN-WE DID A LOT MORE THAN FLIRT

BUT IT'S NOT TRUE WHAT THEY SAY CAUSE ONLY TEN OF EM

    WORKED

A COUPLE DAYS LATER WE GOT SICKER THAN HECK

SO WE WENT TO THE DOCTOR TO GET OURSELVES CHECKED

HE SAID I HAD THE HEPITITIS A THROUGH E

BUT MY WIFE HAD CAUGHT THE HEPITITIS B THROUGH T

OUR SKIN TURNED GREEN THEN A REAL PRETTY YELLER

ALL FROM EAT'IN OYSTERS THAT ROCKED A FELLER

BRAISED & BUTTERED BEEF BRAINS

I HIT A BIG BRAMA BULL WITH MY BUICK ONE MORNING

IT WALKED OUT IN THE ROAD WITHOUT ANY WARNING

IT WAS BEATEN AND BATTERED INTO DELICIOUS SUBMISSION

BUT IT TORE OFF MY STARTER AND RUINED MY TRANSMISSION

I GATHERED UP ALL OF THE BEEF PARTS I COULD

AND LAID IT ALL OUT ON WHAT WAS LEFT OF MY HOOD

THIS BEEF LOOKED LIKE IT HAD BEEN HIT BY A TRAIN

BUT ONE PART INTACT THAT WAS LEFT WAS IT'S BRAIN

SO I TOOK IT AND SLICED IT AND BRAISED IT WITH BUTTER

IT WAS CREAMY AND BEEFY AND I SHARED WITH MY MOTHER

DEER SLIDERS

IT'S NOT GOT TO DO WITH HOW YA FRY'EM OR GRILL'EM

BUT IT'S A REAL FANCY WAY ABOUT HOW YOU CAN KILL'EM

YA NEED A GREAT BIG CAR IT DON'T MATTER WHAT KIND

A CHEVY OR AN OLDSMOBILE - WHATEVER YOU CAN FIND

YOU'LL NEED A CUTT'IN TORCH A HAMMER AND A PILE OF

    SCRAP METAL

A FOUR BARREL CARB AND A MERGENCY BRAKE PEDAL

BUILD KINDA LIKE A WHEELY BAR, ABOUT KNEE HIGH TO A DEER

WELD A SPOILER ON YOUR TRUNK AND DRINK YOURSELF SOME

    BEER

SO WHEN YOUR OUT THERE DRIV'IN AND YOU SEE A DEER UP

    THERE

JUST HIT YOUR BRAKE AND SPIN AROUND SO YOUR SPOILER

    CATCHES AIR

AND IF YOU HAD YOUR TRUNK UNLOCKED IT'LL OPEN REALLY

    QUICK

I HOPE DRINK'IN BEER AND SPINN'N ROUND DOES'NT MAKE YOU

    SICK

THIS ONLY WORKS FOR DEER YA KNOW - IT'S NO GOOD FOR A

    LITTLE SKUNK

JUST HIT THE DEER ABOUT THE KNEES AND IT LANDS RIGHT IN

    YOUR TRUNK

TOM CAT - TOM FLAT

I SQUASHED A LITTLE KITTYCAT — DOGGONE SHAME

FLAT AS A PANCAKE AND STUCK TO THE FRAME

RIGHT BESIDE THE MANIFOLD IT COOKS REAL SLOW

DEPENDING ON THE WEATHER AND HOW FAST YA GO

TO GET HIM DONE IN THE MIDDLE YA GOTTA TIME IT JUST RIGHT

IT TAKES AN HOUR IN THE DAY AND TWO OF THE NIGHT

BUT IF YOU'RE LIKE ME AND LIKE YOUR TOM CATS RARE

JUST REV UP YOUR MOTOR AND DON'T GO ANYWHERE

IF YOU'VE GOT A FOUR BARREL CARB WITH DUAL EXHAUST PIPES

IT'S HARD TO GET YOUR TOM CAT COOKED JUST RIGHT

WHEN IT'S DONE THE WAY YOU LIKE IT AND YOU'RE READY TO EAT

CUT THE HEAD AND THE TAIL OFF AND ALL FOUR FEET

ADD A SLICE OF JACK CHEESE AND SOME WHOLE WHEAT BREAD

IT'S A SHAME TO EAT A CAT BUT HE'S ALREADY DEAD

POSSUM ON AN OAK PLANK

TAKE A NORMAL SIZED POSSUM THAT'S BOUGHT THE FARM

PUT HIM ON A HOOK AND HANG HIM IN THE BARN

LET THE SMELL OF THE COW DUNG RISE UP THROUGH

LET HIM CURE THAT WAY FOR A MONTH OR TWO

GO TO THE WOODS AND CUT A GREEN OAK BOARD

THEN HEAD FOR THE BARN WHERE THE POSSUM WAS STORED

BY NOW THE AROMA WILL BE TRULY AWESOME

HOLD DOWN THE PLANK AND NAIL ON THE POSSUM

NO SENSE IN FIGHTIN OR PUSHIN OR SHOVIN

JUST WASH UP YOUR HANDS AND PREHEAT THE OVEN

COOK IN THE OVEN TILL MEDIUM RARE

LEAVE ON THE TAIL AND ALL OF THE HAIR

FOR THIS FINE SUPPER YOU'VE GOT ME TO THANK

SCRAPE OFF THE POSSUM AND EAT THE PLANK

REAL
"WILD GAME"
RECIPES

REAL "WILD GAME" RECIPES

POSSUM CASSEROLE

1 possum
1 onion
1 clove garlic
clarified butter
olive oil (enough to brown meat
    without becoming dry)
1 cup dry red wine

flat or field mushroom, sliced (big meaty ones)
2 tablespoons fresh herbs (a mix of rosemary,
    thyme, marjoram, dill and parsley)
1 tablespoon tomato puree
1 cup dark beer, eg black mac, monteiths
1 cup brown possum stock
1 tablespoon marsala

Skin and bone the possum (use only the best meat for the casserole, ie: the strip loins and hind quarters, cubed). Reserve the carcass and trimmings for stock. In a heavy pan, heat the clarified butter and oil. Sauté onion and garlic.

When onion is clear, remove to casserole. Dust the cubed possum with flour and brown in batches. Add to casserole. Melt a little more clarified butter and sauté bacon and mushrooms. Remove to casserole De-glaze pan as necessary with red wine- add this to casserole together with herbs, ground pepper, tomato purée, beer and marsala. Stir, cover and cook in slow oven for 2-3 hours, adding more possum stock if necessary.

HOW TO CATCH A POSSUM

Since some recipes here involve possum, I figured it might be worth it to include a section on how to get your hands on one. I know of several ways to catch a possum. Perhaps the easiest is to simply drive around for a while in your truck. The problem will soon resolve itself. (SCCRRRREEEEECCHHH!!. . . SPLAT. . .)

Much more fun, however, is to take your dogs and shotgun, and go into the woods and hunt one down. The advantage to this method is that you don't have to scrape the possum off the pavement. The disadvantage is that you do have to worry about shotgun pellets in the meat. (OUCH! Dadgum it! There went my best tooth!)

Not to mention that a shotgun blast can really mess up the hide, which makes it a lot harder for the taxidermist.

It is also possible to set traps to catch a possum, but this method is notoriously unreliable. Possums like to stay in the trees, and you're much more likely to catch something else. (Hey, Ed! There's something in the trap! See them bushes moving? Let's see what it is! . . . OH, $#&@! IT'S A SKUNK!!)

Another thing you might want to take into consideration is that possums are scavengers. They eat anything. If a possum is in the road, chances are he's there looking for lunch. Therefore, it's best to catch them alive if at all possible and feed them corn for a few days to clean them out real good before eating them. You just don't know whose garbage they've been into. After all, you wouldn't want to eat something that's been eating Aunt Edna's leftovers, would you? You know, she's the one who brings that stuff that nobody ever touches to the family reunion.

(Hey, man, what IS that stuff? I think it's still alive!)

Possums are also notoriously hard to kill, and they, well, play possum if they feel threatened. (That's why they're called possums!) I remember hearing about someone who had a possum get in his garage one time. He was real mad about something, and having a possum rooting around in his garage making a mess just made it worse, so he took after that thing with a shovel. The possum never had a chance.

He did have to chop its head off to make sure it was dead; otherwise they just get up and walk off. It was real strange; right after he beheaded the possum, lightning or something struck the garage, blowing out all the lightbulbs and giving him quite a shock. (If you don't get the joke here, don't worry.)

Please note that we're talking about the North American opossum here. There is a species of possum (spelled without the leading "o") native to Australia which is endangered. It is strictly illegal to hunt, trap, or kill an Australian possum. However, this same species is reportedly a nuisance in New Zealand, so if you see one there. . . bon appetit!

Of course, if you take this page seriously anyway... you might be a redneck. That ought to get you started. Now, on to the recipes...

WILD POSSUM KABOB

1 Still breathing, corn-fed Possum
3 Ripe but firm tomatoes
1 Large white or yellow onion
1/2 pound large mushrooms

2 large green peppers
1 package meat marinade
1/2 cup soy sauce
12 skewers (sticks are okay in Arkansas)

The possum must be alive so that you can scare it, giving you the "wild" taste from all the adrenaline it produces. It is best to hit it over the head with a large object in a humane manner. Boil the possum for 3 minutes to loosen the fur then skin and gut it.

De-limb (chop the little knubby legs off) the possum and cut the meat into 1/2 inch square chunks.

Marinate overnight in a mixture of meat marinade and soy sauce. Kentucky residents who have no fridge can use an ice chest and may use radiator coolant instead of soy sauce.

Thread the meat and veggies onto your skewer/stick in alternating sequences to distribute the delicious flavor evenly.

Cook over a barbecue, pit, 50 gallon drum or any other fire till you get the desired result. For added flavor, you can cook it over burning tires.

POSSUM AND TATERS

1 young, fat possum
8 sweet potatoes
2 tablespoons butter

1 tablespoon sugar
salt

First, catch a possum. This in itself is excellent entertainment on a moonlight night. Skin the possum and remove the head and feet. Be sure to wash it thoroughly. Freeze overnight either outside or in a refrigerator.

When ready to cook, peel the potatoes and boil them tender in lightly salted water along with the butter and sugar. At the same time, stew the possum tender in a tightly covered pan with a little water. Arrange the taters around the possum, strip with bacon, sprinkle with thyme or marjoram, or pepper, and brown in the oven. Baste often with the drippings.

ARMADILLO IN MUSTARD SAUCE

1 1/4 cups dry white wine
1/2 cup oil
2 garlic cloves, crushed (optional)
1/4 cup butter
Salt and pepper to taste
1/2 tsp. thyme
1/2 tsp. rosemary

1 med. onion, sliced thin
1 armadillo, cleaned and cut into serving pieces
1 1/4 cups light cream
1 tbsp. brown mustard (e.g. Gulden's)
    or Poupon Dijon
1 tbsp. cornstarch

Mix all ingredients of marinade and add armadillo. Marinate about 8 hrs., turning meat occasionally. Remove armadillo and reserve marinade.

Melt butter in deep skillet and brown armadillo pieces. Pour in marinade and bring to a boil. Stir in seasoning, cover and simmer until tender (about 1 - 1 1/4 hours.) Remove skillet from the fire and place armadillo pieces on a warmed platter.

Mix mustard and cornstarch, then mix in cream. Return skillet to low heat and stir in this mixture a little at a time. Stir sauce until hot, but not boiling, and thickened. Pour sauce over armadillo. Serve with steamed rice.

ARMADILLO AND RICE

1 armadillo, dressed and cleaned
4 large onions
1 stalk celery
2 cans chopped mushrooms

2 cups rice, uncooked
Salt and pepper to taste
10 cups armadillo broth

Boil armadillo until tender; reserve broth. Remove meat from bones. Cut onions and celery and cook in butter until tender. Add mushrooms and meat and simmer for 5 minutes. Put in a large baking pan or dutch oven and add 10 cups of hot broth; add rice, salt and pepper; stir. Place in 375 degrees F. oven and cook until tender.

COUNTRY-STYLE GROUNDHOG

7 individual groundhogs
½ cup flour
¼ tsp. salt
¼ tsp. pepper

¼ tsp. soda
¼ c. cooking oil
½ tsp. sugar

Prepare groundhog by removing the small sacs in the back and under the forearm. Soak groundhog overnight in salted water. This will help remove the gamey flavor. Combine flour, salt, pepper, and soda; use as a rub on the groundhog. Brown the groundhog in hot oil in the skillet, and sprinkle with sugar. Reduce heat, add 1 ½ cup water. Cover, simmer for about 30 minutes or until tender. Remove cover; let cook for an additional 10 minutes.

BAKED GROUND HOG

Ground Hog
Spicewood branches
Salt, pepper to taste

Flour
Bacon grease or ½ cup shortening

Dress and cut the groundhog. Bring water to a boil on the stove, and then place the groundhog in boiling water. Break spicewood branches, and but into the pot. Continue boiling until groundhog is tender. Remove groundhog from pot. Season with salt and pepper, then roll in flour and bacon grease. Put in oven and bake until golden brown.

ORIENTAL GROUNDHOG

1 groundhog
2 quarts water
¼ cup salt
½ cup soy sauce
2 whole cloves garlic
1 whole pepper
¼ onion

2 tablespoon mild chile powder
¼ bunch whole parsley
4 beef bouillon cubes
¼ teaspoon freshly-ground white pepper
1 cup beef or chicken broth
Teriyaki glaze

Cut meat into pieces and let soak in 1 quart water and salt for three hours. Transfer groundhog to 1 quart fresh water and soak 4 hours. Drain and dry meat. Place meat in a baking pan with broth, soy sauce, garlic cloves, pepper, onion, Chile powder, parsley, bullion cubes, and white pepper. Cover and bake at 350 degrees for an hour to an hour and a half. Baste frequently and finish with teriyaki glaze.

Groundhog and Sweet Potatoes

Groundhog
Cold water
Salt

Pepper
Sweet potatoes or white potatoes
Cornbread

Dress the groundhog as quickly as possible, and let soak for several hours in cold, salty water. After the meat is cold, you can trim any excess fat. Parboil to remove any remaining fat. Drain well. Place in oven at medium temperature with potatoes. Season the meat with salt and pepper and bake until brown.

Baked Squirrel

4 cut up squirrels (use only hind legs
    and meaty back pieces)
1 chopped green pepper
2 Tbsp butter
4 Tbsp. red wine
1 can cream of mushroom soup
1/4 c. vinegar

1 chopped onion
4 Tbsp. salt
1 tsp. Adolph's tenderizer
1 tsp. pepper
1 c. flour
Crisco and cooking oil

Mix vinegar and salt with water to cover squirrel. Soak 2 hours in solution. Remove pieces and shake on tenderizer and pepper. Roll in flour. Fry in Crisco until brown. Place pieces in baking dish. In another skillet saute onion and pepper in butter. Add wine and soup. Mix well. Pour over squirrel. Bake at 350 degrees for 30 minutes.

Country Style Squirrel

2 squirrels
Salt & pepper to taste
Flour

6 tbsp. vegetable oil
2 c. water

Cut squirrel into frying size pieces, salt and pepper then roll in flour until coated well. Put in skillet of hot oil and fry until golden. Remove squirrel and most the oil, then add water and bring to boil. Place squirrel back into the skillet, turn to low heat, cover and cook for approximately 1 hour.

Oven Fried Squirrel

One squirrel
4 eggs
bread crumbs
Flour

Olive oil
Canola oil/ vegetable oil
Butter

Pat meat dry with paper towel to remove any moisture. Dip squirrel in egg. Combine bread crumbs with flour, dip egg-covered squirrel in mix. Cover bottom of skillet with olive oil and canola oil, add butter and brown meat well (about 20 min). Put squirrel in baking dish and pour contents of skillet over meat. Bake for one hour at 375°F.

BELGIAN SQUIRREL

3 large squirrels
1/2 cup butter
2 onions, sliced
3 tablespoons white vinegar
1/8 teaspoon dried thyme

salt and pepper to taste
18 pitted prunes
1 1/2 teaspoons all-purpose flour
1 cup cold water

Clean squirrels. Burn away any fur that clings. Rinse the meat though several changes of water and pat dry. Cut squirrels into serving pieces.

Preheat the oven to 375 degrees F. Melt the butter in a large skillet over medium heat. Add squirrel pieces and fry until browned on all sides, but do not cook through. Remove the squirrel pieces to a large Dutch oven or oven safe crock. Add onions to the butter in the skillet; cook and stir until tender and browned. Pour the onions and butter into the pot with the squirrel. Fill with enough water to almost cover the meat. Mix in the vinegar and season with thyme, salt and pepper. Cover and place in the oven.

Bake for 45 minutes in the preheated oven. Remove the pot from the oven and add the prunes. Return to the oven and reduce the heat to 325 degrees F. Continue baking for another 45 minutes.

Remove the pot from the oven. Mix the flour and cold water together in a cup. Use a slotted spoon to remove the meat and prunes to a serving dish. Set the pot on the stove and bring to a boil over medium-high heat. Stir in the flour and water and simmer, stirring constantly, until the gravy is thick enough to coat a metal spoon. Serve meat with a lot of gravy.

SQUIRREL COUNTRY SAUSAGE

4 ½ lbs. squirrel (approx. 15
    fox squirrels)
1 Tbsp. sage
2 lbs. fresh seasoned pork
    sausage (with sage)
2 tsp. basil
1 onion

3 tsp. margarine
3 cloves garlic
1 Tbsp. chili powder
4 Tbsp. fresh parsley
1 Tbsp. black pepper
2 Tbsp. salt
1 tsp. thyme

De-bone the squirrel and chop in food processor. Mix together with fresh pork. Mince the onion and garlic. Cook the onion until transparent and add the garlic and sauté slightly. Mix together meats, onion, garlic and herbs.

To test seasonings, form a small patty and fry in frying pan with butter. Taste and adjust seasonings accordingly.

Form into small patties to cook or grill and use with your favorite sausage recipes. Great on pizza, with pancakes or scrambled in eggs.

Squirrel can be a delightful little meal and will maybe make your yard a bit quieter. Enjoy!

Grilled Venison Backstrap Supreme

I covet venison backstrap as much as Ebenezer Scrooge coveted money. There is so much meat from a big deer and so little of those tender, tasty backstraps that one hates to cook them poorly.

In summer, we barbecue a lot, and backstraps on the grill are the centerpiece of one of our favorite meals. Here's how we do it.

First, I soak the backstraps in salt water to get every iota of blood out of the meat. Once that's done, I rinse them in cold fresh water and pat them dry. Then I trim all the viscera and fat away, leaving nothing but pure meat.

For this simple recipe you'll need about 2 pounds of backstraps cut into thick little 2-inch chunks. You'll also need a quart of sweet apple cider, 2 pounds of bacon, one large red onion and 24 ounces of your favorite barbecue sauce.

To start, place the venison chunks in a shallow baking dish wide enough to keep from having to pile them on top of each other. Pour the apple cider over them, cover and refrigerate overnight. In the morning, remove the chunks from the cider, pat them dry, and set them aside while you wash and dry the dish. Return the chunks to the dish and cover them with the barbecue sauce, then refrigerate until its time to cook them—at least 3 hours.

Before cooking, take the meat out of the refrigerator and let it warm up to room temperature. While you preheat the grill to high heat, wrap each meat chunk with a slice of bacon and a thin slice of onion, holding it all together with a wooden toothpick. Coat the grill with cooking spray or brush it with olive oil to keep the meat from sticking. Now place the meat onto the grill, making sure there is some air between each chunk. I keep a small squirt bottle of water handy and when the bacon drippings start kicking up flames, squirt them down without putting out my fire. Turn them occasionally until the bacon becomes a little burnt—usually about 20 minutes.

Remove and serve with a fresh salad, garlic toast, fresh asparagus and a chilled Merlot. Bon appetit!

Best Venison Stir Fry Ever

If you take your deer to a professional butcher, chances are, along with those steaks, backstraps, roasts and hamburger he gives you back some chops. Most people broil or grill their chops, and that's a great way to do them up. But for a tasty oriental twist, try stir frying them.

How much meat you need is dependent upon how many people you'll be feeding. I figure about a half pound of meat per person, with my chops about a 1/2- to 3/4-inch thick; the amount of vegetables you use is dependent upon how much your crew likes them. Then I get a whole bunch of fresh carrots, fresh bean sprouts, celery, broccoli, a red bell pepper, a handful of mushrooms, some unsalted peanuts, 1 medium yellow onion and 2 cloves of garlic. You'll also need 1 tbsp. of crushed red pepper, 1 tsp. of ground cumin, a cup of soy sauce and a bit of canola oil.

Continued on page 42

The first step is to marinate the chops in soy sauce overnight in the refrigerator. Then comes the work—prepping the vegetables. That means peeling, then chunking, carrots, slicing celery, cutting broccoli and dicing the garlic and onion. I like to keep everything in separate small cups so it is all handy and easy to grab.

It is best to do the cooking in a large wok, but since I like to keep the bone in my chops I find a very large skillet works best for me. Get the skillet very, very hot, then coat it with just enough canola oil to keep everything from sticking. Cook the meat about 30 seconds per side, then add everything else, including the seasoning. Stir constantly, making sure everything hits the hot skillet and is coated with all the spices and oil. Do not overcook!

Serve with a side of fried rice and, if I am feeling like it, I'll top the stir fry with some of those crunchy cooked noodles you can find in the oriental food section at the store. Wash it down with some icy Tsing Tao beer. This is a low-calorie, low-fat meal that doesn't taste like it.

DEER BURGER KABOB STACKERS

1 lb. Ground venison
1 package string cheese sticks
   (cut into 1" chunks)
1 lb. bacon
1 can biscuit dough

1/2 cup diced onions
1/2 cup diced green peppers
1/2 cup diced mushrooms
1 egg
Salt & pepper to taste

Soak skewers in water for 4 hours. Mix ground venison with diced onions, peppers, mushrooms, and egg in a large mixing bowl. Season venison burger to taste. Roll the venison burger into 1" meatballs. Cut the biscuit dough into chunks and roll into 1/2" balls. Cut the string cheese into 1" chunks or use cheese cubes of your choice.

It's time to assemble your kabobs…place a dough ball on the skewer, then a meatball, followed by cheese, followed by another dough ball. Repeat so that each stick is essentially a double stacked burger. Once kabob is assembled, wrap the entire thing in bacon. Grill until bacon is done. Enjoy a new and fun filled way to eat venison burger.

COON MEAL IN A BAG (RECIPE 1)

1 raccoon, cleaned
1 lb bacon
seasoning salt

pepper
your favorite batter
oil

Make sure all the fat and glands are removed from the coon. Stuff the bacon inside the coon. Season to taste with seasoning salt and pepper.

Pour on the batter and shake to create a thin layer all over. Add to hot oil in a Dutch oven, fish fryer or turkey fryer. Cook until golden brown. Remove and drain.

Allow to cool a few minutes before slicing. Serve and enjoy.

COON MEAL IN A BAG (RECIPE 2)

1 cleaned raccoon
8 medium Irish(red) potatoes,
    peeled and cubed
3 lb bag baby carrots
2 large onions, sliced into 1/2" slices
4 bell peppers, diced

4 medium turnips, quartered
1 can cream of mushroom soup
1 1/2 cups water
2 oz Morton's Natures Seasoning
1 large baking bag, turkey size
electric roasting oven with liner

Place coon in the baking bag. Add the potatoes, carrots, onions, peppers and turnips. Mix the soup and water together in a bowl. Add to bag. Sprinkle on the Morton's seasoning evenly as possible. Seal bag. Put 1 gallon of water in the roaster to make a water bath. Place the bag in the liner and place in roaster. Cook for 6 - 8 hours at 250 degrees. Serve and enjoy. * *You can cook this in the oven if you don't have a roaster. Adjust cooking time as needed.*

BAR-B-Q'D RACCOON

4-6 lb. raccoon, cut into serving pieces
1 cup red wine
2 onions, sliced
3 bay leaves
1 tbsp salt

1 tsp pepper
3 cloves garlic, sliced
2 cups of your favorite barbecue sauce
1 tbsp paprika

Place the raccoon pieces in a large pan. Add the wine, onions, bay leaves, salt, pepper and garlic. Add enough water to cover the meat. Bring to a boil. Cover and simmer for 1 hour.

After 1 hour, remove the meat and drain. Place the raccoon in a greased baking dish. Mix the barbecue sauce and paprika together and pour over the meat. Cook at 325 degrees for 50 - 60 minutes. Serve and Enjoy!

MISSISSIPPE COON STEW

1 skinned, deboned, defatted
    raccoon, cubed
1 large Vidalia onion, diced
3 cloves garlic, crushed
3 medium turnips, diced
2 lbs small whole potatoes

3 stalks celery, diced
1 tsp cayenne pepper
1 tsp salt
1 tsp Old Bay seasoning
1 cup sour cream
4 cups water or enough to cover

Add all of the ingredients to a large cast iron pot. Stir together. Bring to a boil. Cover and simmer 1 1/2 - 2 hours stirring occasionally. Add more water if necessary.

Serve with a side salad, corn pone or cat head biscuits, vegetable of choice and iced tea. Enjoy.

NEW ORLEANS DOVE RECIPE

16 dove breasts, boned
1-1/2 cups bulk spicy Italian sausage
Creole seasoning
1 cup okra
4 cups fresh tomatoes, chopped
1 onion, chopped
2 celery stalks, chopped

1/2 cup green bell pepper, chopped
chicken broth
2 cups raw rice
2 cups shrimp
Creole seasoning, to taste
salt and pepper to taste

In a heavy skillet, sprinkle sausage with creole seasoning and fry until completely cooked. Remove sausage, drain well and place in a dutch oven.

Sprinkle the dove breasts with creole seasoning and brown all sides in the grease; remove place in the dutch oven.

Now add the onion, celery and bell pepper in the sausage grease and fry until tender. Drain and place in dutch oven. Add the tomatoes and enough chicken broth to cover all. Bring to a boil and simmer for a good hour; or until the dove is cooked through. Season again if needed. Add the raw rice and shrimp. Simmer until rice is cooked and serve.

HOW TO EASILY PLUCK A WILD TURKEY

For those of you that wish to try some of my wild turkey recipes and if you want to pluck your turkey I have some simple steps for doing so.

To loosen the feathers - heat a large pan of water until it is very hot and dunk the turkey in the water many times (I do it 15 times or so). If they are still hard to pull, repeat this process again. Pluck the bird just down to the legs and wings - because you will be removing them in the next step.

A lot of hunters just keep skinless, boneless breast meat too. Using a game shears; you now can remove the head, wings and feet. Grab the entrails and pull them out. Place the turkey in a kitchen sink filled with very cold water to cool down the meat.

SNAPPING TURTLE IN A POT

1 to 2 lbs. turtle meat
1/4 c. dry sherry wine (optional)
2 tsp. instant, minced onion
2 carrots, sliced
1/8 tsp. dried basil

Salt
2 c. water
2 celery stalks cut into pieces
8 sm. unpeeled redskinned potatoes, halved

Salt turtle meat well and place in your slow cooking pot. Add all other ingredients in order given. Then cover and cook on low heat for 6 or 7 hours or until turtle meat is tender. Remove turtle meat from to and cut into bite size pieces. Return meat to slow cooking pot, cover, and continue to cook on low heat for an additional 2 hours or until vegetables are done.

WILD BOAR BACON

2 good sized wild boar bellies
2 gallons of water
2 cups sea salt
1/4 cup curing salt (pink salt)
1/4 cup whole peppercorns

1/4 cup garlic powder
1/4 cup onion powder
1/4 cup Worcestershire sauce
1 cup brown sugar

One might say, "How could you start a list withOUT bacon?", and to that person I say, "I know exactly what you mean." Next is a great recipe for how to cure your own wild boar bacon, which is a lot easier than one might imagine.

WILD BOAR RIBS WITH FIG BBQ SAUCE

1 tsp black pepper
1 tsp paprika
1 Tbsp fresh chopped thyme
1-1/4 tsp kosher salt – divided
24 racks St. Louis wild boar ribs
(about 3 lbs)

1-1/4 cups chicken stock
1 bay leaf
3/4 cup fig jam or preserves
3 Tbsp canned tomato sauce
2 Tbsp apple cider vinegar
1/4 to 1/2 tsp ground chipotle pepper

It's not hard to convince someone to come over for dinner; you just have to use the magic word: "ribs". You'll be hard-pressed to find someone who won't enjoy this flavorful dish. The sweetness of the figs creates a luscious BBQ sauce that will ignite your taste buds and enhance the natural flavors of the meat. Try this one on a cold night and pop in a movie while they roast in the oven to peak tenderness.